U

Discovering Your God-Given Identity

By Robert C. Bennett

By Robert Bennett

Cover illustration: Devin McCrey

I dedicate this book to all women throughout the world. I especially like to thank those women who daily push me to be the best man possible. These women pull me closer to my destiny as I push them to the highest heights of maximizing their potential and regaining correct images of themselves. For this, I am truly grateful.

Additional Dedications

To my Lord and Savior Jesus Christ; your transformational power stopped me from living selfishly and through your grace I strive on a daily basis to be a giver. Thank you for trusting me with the job of showing women how much you care for them.

To my spiritual mother Pastor Sonia Badger; I want to thank you for always pushing me to fulfill my potential opposed to allowing me to act immature. I appreciate the manner in which you always told me the truth even when I did not want to hear it. Thank you for being dedicated to building spiritual leaders and visionaries.

To Pastor Gwen Shaw; I want to also thank you for your dedication and perseverance over the years that allowed me to experience a divine appointment. That appointment is transforming my entire life; it has given me this revelation that I hope will empower women and transform minds across the nations.

U R WOMAN

Discovering Your God-Given Identity

Forward

"You Are Woman" is the second book in a four set series designed to help inspire women to maximize their potential and give men an intricate perspective about women from God's point of view. The first book in the series is "Letters to the Women I Love". This book looks at several different female personality types, gives voice to issues faced by many women, and displays the strength and courage found in their perseverance. "You Are Woman" examines women's God-given design and the power that lies within them when they walk in their God-given purpose.

The third upcoming book is named "Issues of Identity." This book will examine a woman's process by comparing scenarios from biblical female characters and displaying the similarities with today's women. Its goal is to show today's female strategies for overcoming similar issues faced by those women of old. The final book in the series will be named "More Letters". This book is an evaluation of the first book from the author's perspective; it answers some of the questions that readers have asked me about the first book, and offers readers an opportunity to engage in a deeper discussion with regards to women, men, and relationships.

"You Are Woman" is not just a dramatic piece of literature; it is designed to help women discover and walk in their true identity. It contains "Golden Nuggets" to meditate on, and "Declarations" to be spoken over your life. Please use this book as a foundational tool on your journey to maximizing your full potential as you discover your TRUE identity in God.

Robert C Bennett

LIONESS

A **lioness** is a female lion. Lionesses are the core members of, and the primary hunters for each primary social group of lions. They are known as alpha, super, or top-level predators. This simply means that they have no predators of their own, residing at the top of their food chain. They have a crucial role in maintaining the health of their ecosystems.

They are also considered keystone species; they play a critical role in maintaining the structure of a natural community and whose impact on the community is **greater** than would be expected based on its relative abundance or total biomass.

INTRODUCTION

As I continue my work in what I believe to be my "God" given calling (which is motivating women to maximize their full potential), I am becoming increasingly aware of the quantity of women struggling with incorrect images of themselves. The major challenge I face in my daily work is trying to convince women that they are designed with greatness in them, and this greatness is given to them by God.

As I continue my Male Maturity Development Process (MMDP), I am becoming more conscious and sensitive to women issues and their inner struggles. What I mean by this is I have developed a "God" given sensitivity to women, so it usually does not take long in a conversation for me to engage the secret parts of a woman's psyche. I am very mindful of my "gift" so I always guard the anointing and insight given to me with careful honor.

I understand that any variance from the mindset of helping is very dangerous, so I don't take my "gift" lightly. I keep myself conscious of this "divine" insight, because it gives me the potential to damage women's lives opposed to helping them heal; and being an agent of healing is my genuine desire. My daily prayer is; "God keep me humble and give me more insight with regards to understanding these revelations, so that I can continue helping women transform."

As I am writing and sharing these concepts, the revelations continue to come, which causes the information to evolve. As I gain more revelation about God's view of women, I become more & more eager to share what I am receiving.

This book is designed to set a solid foundation for **YOU** to build upon: it is only a means to an end, and not an end itself. It is very probable that I will gain more insight once I have completed this endeavor, so I will do my best to stay on target and express what is necessary for you to get a clear understanding of the truths that will be revealed.

Although it may seem as though I am writing a book designed for women, I honestly believe that this book contains very strong and helpful revelation that will also assist men. There are universal implications to every line and precept presented. If you are a man reading this, please allow yourself the opportunity to go through the Male Maturity Development process: it will enhance every relationship that you have with any woman in your life.

REFLECTION

In the midst of getting this revelation about women, I questioned God "why me?" I had two failed marriages and have not been what would be considered the most "lucky" in relationships. As a matter of fact, my history with women would seem to disqualify me from ever being able to speak out in regards to female concepts whatsoever. But, I heard His voice telling me "it is because of the mistakes that you have corrected that I can now trust you." The message that I have is not the most popular; it may be especially hard for some, because it challenges traditional thinking. But, I challenge you to consider the concepts presented for in them lies wisdom and blessings.

Because this revelation is so dynamic I wanted to publish quickly; after all, who wouldn't want to get the truth out there fast? I was very interested in people discovering the truth that could launch them into their destiny. For some reason, it just didn't work out the way I wanted it. I realized that God had so much more to say about the subject matter. This forced me to slow down and as one friend would advise me, "some things you must let simmer Rob".

My goal is for you to hear the very voice of God echoed through my writing. It is important to fully examine each concept (simmer). It is only through stepping out of tradition and engaging in real conversation on taboo topics that we promote a true understanding of each other. I hope that this book encourages richer conversations on the subject matter of God's view of women, and I hope it promotes a more thorough research of the concepts presented.

It is expected that new ideas and concepts will spring forth while you are reading this information. God's thoughts are above our thoughts and His ways are above our ways. I hope that I free myself in a manner that will allow me to express the words that God wants to use to empower women. I pray that this book will assist women and men with understanding women's God-given identity.

When I started this prayerful journey, I thought I was trying to help women transform into something "new". What I mean by that statement is that my predominant desire is to see women come out of the stereotypical concepts that have been historically and traditionally placed upon them. But, the revelation I received is I do not need to focus on history or tradition, but I need to see HIS-story if I am going to help women see their **ORIGINAL** design: women and men whom embrace the **TRUTH** concerning this will automatically respond in a "new" way.

My hope is when I display the truths that have been revealed to me concerning women's ORIGINAL design, purpose, and destiny; the revelations I am receiving will speak to them as emphatically as it explodes in my heart. If you get nothing else out of what you read, the most crucial thing is **GOD LOVES YOU!**

He has a destiny for you, which does not rely on any limited definition or "box" that someone believes you should be in because you are a woman. God designed you as a perfect creation; there is no biblical record of anything ever being "taken" out of you.

From the beginning, women were created so complete, that God was able to rest after the female arrived on the scene! Your identity is wrapped up in Him. You have a wonderful image that is honorable, strong, and beautiful: **YOU ARE WOMAN!**

SIMPLY CONVERSATING

I was sitting down with my sister one Sunday afternoon and we began discussing my first book "Letters to the Women I Love". She was complimenting me for taking a risk to examine women's processes. She had questions concerning certain aspects of the book, but was very impressed with the way she believed I had poured my heart out across the pages. She made a statement that was a common thread among many women who had read that book. Her definitive statement was "I found myself on many of the pages".

She had recently gotten engaged and was entering the final stages of getting ready for marriage. As the conversation progressed, she expressed feeling troubled by some of the things that was going on in her relationship, and wished her fiancé would read the book prior to them "tying" the knot. She felt like his demeanor was simply hard and rough, plus he wanted her to compromise some principles that she had recently placed in her life. Before I could pull the words back into my mouth, I had made a statement that was a little shocking to both of us, but had a true tone to it: **A MAN HAS NO EXPERIENCE IN BECOMING A BRIDE**!

We both just stared at each other for a moment as to say "where did that come from?" It was such a revolutionary thought that it drove us into a deep level of conversation. The truth is I had never even considered this fact before we had this conversation. This is a concept that I am still gaining revelation about, and I am still in the process of digesting all of the pieces that go along with the "becoming a bride" statement.

Since God used me to make a statement like that, I ask Him to give me insight into the statement. I knew at that very moment I was about to go on a journey that would increase my understanding of women. I know this statement may seem strange, especially after viewing all of the information that I stated earlier. I am aware of the uncommon call on my life; and because of my professional work which has caused me to development as a man, I thought that I knew something about a woman's process. It was sad to have to admit that I had little insight to the female's original design; although I have been told that I am much further along than most men.

Just to put things in its proper perspective; I have spent 40 plus hours per week, for the last 5 years, as the central figure responsible for an average of 70 women per year. That's approximately 10,400 hours spent around 350 distinct personalities, and I still did NOT have the insights that I will be sharing across the pages.

What I will be sharing with you is under the direct inspiration of the Holy Spirit. I asked Him to reveal the true identity of women to me, so I can properly assist them in reclaiming their destiny. What you will read is exactly what He showed me. When you tap into your God-given identity, there isn't anything that you cannot accomplish. Listen to the Holy Spirit as He reveals your Identity to you.

DIVINE VISITATION

It was a Wednesday afternoon and I was still at work, but I was really looking forward to leaving on time that day. Wednesday nights I play basketball and I try not to let anything interfere. It is the only activity that I'm involved in that gives me true peace of mind: when I'm on the court I am not thinking about anything else. When my "spiritual" mother calls me and says "I have someone I want you to meet;" all I can think is "there goes my plans." But, I have learned to tune into the spirit of God in her; so I settle it in my heart that I would not be playing basketball that day.

What I did not realize is that this was the answer to my prayer. I didn't realize that I was about to experience a divine visitation that would change my life forever. I will never forget the experience; we went to a service in a house, the atmosphere was electric, and there was a very high expectation that God was going to meet us there. I met an elderly woman name Pastor Gwen Shaw; she was not loud or animated, but very much anointed. She began to tell us about her life and the many things that she had to experience as a female evangelist.

The service began at approximately 7pm and did not end until about 2am. As we were leaving, Pastor Shaw called me over and made me kneel while she placed her hands on my shoulders as a king would do to a knight that he was about to anoint for a mission. I will never forget the prophecy she gave me "God has called you into the world and a son, to show the love of the Father to women.

Since that moment, I have received revelations that have been explosive to my mind: this is what has been revealed, if you apply these concepts you will be successful.

BIRTHING PROCESS

Before we get into the meat of the book, God revealed to me an experience that is very common to women, but rarely examined in detail: He had me study the birthing process. As I was following His direction, I began wondering "what is so important about the birthing process?" God made it clear that to come out of the traditional mindset about women you will have to go through the proper stages of birth, or it will just be another good book, and piece of information gained with no results. Let's examine the birthing process in detail to see why it is so important to the journey you are going to undertake.

There are 4 stages to the birthing process: labor onset to full cervix dilation, full cervix dilation to delivery of the baby, delivery of the baby to expulsion of the placenta, and expulsion of the placenta to afterbirth recovery.

STAGE 1:
Labor Onset to Full Cervix Dilation
This stage consists of **regular uterine contractions** with cervix dilation. The length of this stage varies from mother to mother. It depends on many factors including but not limited to previous pregnancies, the health and condition of the mother and fetus, patience of the doctor (or midwife) and willingness to induce labor, medications used at this stage, hospital versus home birth, etc.

God is saying that you should not get disturb and distracted because you feel the **pressure** of acting on the information that you are receiving. These "**contractions**" are getting you prepared to walk through the process of regaining your "**powerful**" destiny.

19

STAGE 2:
Full Cervix Dilation to Delivery of Baby

During this time, uterine contractions strengthen and become more frequent. During this stage, the mother will feel the need to bear down and push. The baby goes through a series of passive movements - especially the head, which undergoes flexion, internal rotation, extension, external rotation, and crowning (the first sign of the baby's head).

As you continue to get ready to reveal who you are things may get more intense, you may lose relationships, things in your life may get crazy, and so on. These situations are designed to get your **identity** in the correct position for birth.

STAGE 3:
Delivery of Baby to Expulsion of Placenta

This stage consists of the period immediately following birth to the expulsion of the placenta - The placenta should always be examined to be sure no parts remain within the uterus. This can become detrimental to the mother causing hemorrhage and/or death.

Have you ever wondered why people start off well and then it all seems to fall apart? It is because they often stop once they may have seen the dream (baby) come to fruition, forgetting that there is an afterbirth process. Just like in the natural, having the baby will be much simpler than raising and nurturing that child. It is after the baby is born that the real work begins.

God wants to give you insight through examining this stage. It is very important for you to put every concept into your daily life; every component must be realized and there can be no concepts that are not acted upon. If you are going to regain your identity, no "fallen" perspectives can remain. Failure to complete the entire process will cause death to your identity, and you will fall back into the shadows of tradition and complacency.

STAGE 4:
Expulsion of Placenta to Afterbirth Recovery

During this stage, the mother is monitored to be sure no uterine bleeding or other complications occur. God wants you to understand your identity and walk in it. He never wants you to go back into a situation that does not fully maximize your potential as a woman. It is necessary for you to make sure that this is not just a phase in your life, but a transition into your purpose, destiny, and God-given design.

COMPLICATIONS DURING BIRTHING PROCESS

Now that we have examined the stages that you must go through to birth your destiny, let's take a look at the areas that may cause you to fail. As you are walking towards birthing your destiny you are subject to facing several types of complications; Insufficient Power, Passage Obstruction, Baby Mal-positions, Forceps Delivery, and Cesarean Section.

Insufficient Power

Sufficient power and coordinated contractions are essential for a smooth, uncomplicated labor. When the power of the contractions is **weak** or the pattern of contractions **disorganized**, the mother is more likely to become exhausted. This can cause fetal distress resulting in fetal harm and/or c-section.

The entire goal of this book is to assist you with recognizing your original design and power. The challenges that you may face as you are coming into your true identity are the contractions that are getting you strong enough to correctly birth your destiny.

You must learn how to take the disorganized items in your life and bring them into order. It is the challenges that you overcome that will give you the sufficient power necessary to exercise your authority as a woman. You are **powerful**! So, allow the contractions to develop you into the person that you were originally designed to be.

Obstructions

Passage way obstructions (pelvic, uterine, cervix, etc.) can complicate the birthing process. These include tumors, cysts, and fractures. A tumor is a growth that does not belong; and God wants to free you from anything that does not belong in your life. A cyst is a sore; and God wants to move all the sore spots out of your life, and a fracture is a break; which god wants to mend all the breaks in your life.

There are other areas of the birthing process that have relevance to seizing your real identity. They are worth mentioning, but I will not expound on them all; I will leave that as a homework assignment for you to explore, then you can take the revelations that you get and make them applicable to your life.

There is subluxation (a partial dislocation of bones that leave them misaligned but still in some contact with each other; flat male-like pelvis (android), and physiological changes (degenerative joint disease, tuberculosis, rickets).

You can also find your identity in a malposition. Malposition birth presentations include: upside down, breech, face presentation, and forceps delivery.

Before I leave the birthing process concepts and go into explaining your original design, I want to spend a little time on forceps delivery. In the event, there is fetal or mother distress or the labor is not going as planned, forceps assistance may be used. As forceps can cause a number of problems, forceps should only be used in urgent situations.

Some of you may need to get away from dangerous situations. This is necessary if you are going to obtain a victorious life. You may have to go to a place of safety, for example, a shelter or rehab etc., this is a forceps delivery.

Understand that the choice to leave and regain your identity may be a very dangerous time in your life, especially if you are in a domestic violence situation. But, you must make a plan to get out of situations that zap the life out of you, strip you of all positive energy, and prevent you from realizing your power as a woman.

To conclude this chapter I want to touch on Cesarean Section. Although c-sections were becoming very fashionable, experts are now advising steering clear of this course of action except when the mother or fetus is in danger of considerable distress. This is due to the invasiveness of the procedure, and unnecessary stresses placed on the baby.

God wants you to experience the process of fully birthing what it means to be "**WOMAN**" into your world. Every stage that you go through is crucial to you regaining your identity. You will have to go through each stage if you are going to live according to your original design. If you have resolved in your heart that you are going to complete the process; continue reading. You are headed on the adventure of a lifetime: **YOU ARE WOMAN**!

NEW THING!

GOD IS NOT TRYING TO DO A NEW THING!

I know this statement is controversial, but that is simply because everyone seems to be looking for the next new thing. We look for new clothes, gimmicks, fads, and movements. We have the i-phone, 4G, virtual worlds etc. Everything is about getting the latest information and getting it fast. The first concept that God exposed to me is "I am not doing a new thing Rob."

I was extremely puzzled by this statement, because I constantly hear people say "God is doing a new thing in your life". Quite frankly I can't remember hearing anyone teaching what was being revealed to me, so it had to be new. The Holy Spirit then said to me "the last new thing I did was establish the new covenant." God is not trying to get you into something new; He is trying to get you to your **ORIGNAL** purpose!"

> *When Jesus therefore had received the vinegar he said **IT IS FINISHED!** (John 19:30 KJV)*

God's plan has always been getting us back to our **original purpose**. He completed everything that He had to do when Christ gave his life on the cross. From this point forward, if God is going to do a "**NEW**" thing it will line up with getting us to accept **ALL** of our privileges under the "**NEW**" covenant!

I draw your attention to this pivotal point because of the attack that you may experience as a woman when you come into the knowledge of your true identity. You must fully accept that this is not something new or you may fall back into mediocrity.

25

You are only acting in accordance with your original design, so you must press forward despite any opposition. The full expression of your identity is when you begin to act on **ALL** of the privileges that are rightfully yours under the new covenant. This standard is central to fulfilling your destiny, so be confident in this concept.

IDENTITY

Many women that I have met in my life up to this point have lost their sense of identity. Other women have been stripped before they could gain a sense of identity at all (this does not account for those across the world that I have never crossed paths). The enemy has positioned himself to leave women in this condition because of the threat that they pose to him. He attacked your image from the very beginning. The enemy's plan is to make you chase after all types of things that you believe will give you a greater sense of identity.

He does not care what he uses to leave you in a dormant condition, but it normally follows this pattern; inside/outside image (beauty), a man, or drama (traumatic events). Many women spend enormous amounts of time focused on these three aspects of life. There is nothing wrong with the first two aspects as long as it does not create an identity in which you lose your true power. Understand that traumatic events are strategically design by your enemy to strip you of all power.

I was genuinely taken back to find so many women consumed with defining themselves in these three life areas. I have to admit I was even more surprised to see that they came from all levels of life. It did not matter if they were rich, poor, smart, or pretty; from the lowest alley of a city, or elite mansion on a hill. Many women are so distracted by the events name in the preceding paragraph that they miss their true power and God given identity. This same "identity" crisis is leaving many women in some very unfortunate situations.

Many women continue to find themselves in very precarious predicaments lacking any real fulfillment whatsoever. This is a result of incorrect socialization and teaching from the bible. God wants to straighten this "mess" out and bring women back into their predestined identity. This book is simply a tool to start the process.

A warning before you read any further; the information you are about to be exposed to is going to put you face to face with your true enemy (the devil), and he will do anything within his power to keep you from maximizing your full potential. You have a responsibility to act on the information you are exposed to, and as a result revolutionize your world. If you are not ready for the challenge gently **PUT THE BOOK DOWN NOW**!

If you are reading this next paragraph, I assume you are ready to have your mind revolutionized. The words and concepts that you will be exposed to from this point onward will challenge everything that you may have learned. This may put you at odds with anyone who is not interested in you coming into your real identity. If you are a "non-believer" my foundation is not meant to offend you, but it is my belief that many of the systems that have been created to hinder women originated from a misinterpretation of the book of Genesis in the Bible.

This is my primary reason for not offering ANY apologies for relying on the Bible as my source of authority; I believe it reveals all truth about life and empowering women, so you will see scripture referenced throughout the pages. Let's begin:

WHAT IS THE ISSUE?

It all began during a scene in Genesis (Book of Beginnings) in which the female was confronted with a situation that seems to shape the current image we continue to hold in our minds today. She should have not been depicted in a substandard manner, but the enemy came up with a plan that inaccurately displays the woman in a way designed to keep her impotent against him. For centuries, the catastrophic event labeled the "fall of man" has been used as a source of authority for giving women a "lower" position. This stance has caused many women to take a "back seat" to who they truly are in God's eyesight.

The devil fooled us by getting us to scratch the surface of the scriptures, instead of grasping the full revelation that God gave us with regards to looking at women on a deeper level. Part of the enemy's plot was to get us to forget how essential women are to end-time ministry. He did this so they would not be able to give the church valuable insight on "**getting ready**" to become the "**Bride**" of Christ.

The other part of the devil's plan was to give women a "second place" citizenship, so they would never actualize their power against him; this was never God's plan for the woman. The enemy used man's "fallen" condition to declare that the woman was lower than she should be; this was **NOT GOD'S** design. It is **CRITICAL** for us to glean from the woman's knowledge as we properly prepare for the second coming of Christ.

This does not take away from a man's position, because in Christ, there is no race or gender; it simply gives us insight from a different perspective that will assist the entire body with advancing the kingdom.

God designed this age as the time for women to come to the forefront especially in ministry because (1) There was a declaration made over her life; (2) The unique insight that she has in regards to becoming a bride, remember:

A MAN HAS NO EXPERIENCE IN BECOMING A BRIDE!

This is unique to the woman's experience, and God is highlighting this dynamic to the body and beyond, so we can come into a balanced knowledge of one of our primary responsibilities; **preparing for the marriage supper of the lamb**.

NOT GOOD

I need to spell this out, so women can leave the "fallen" perspective of image behind and begin to see themselves from "God's" perspective. If you are a male reading this, you will become very conscious of how prosperous you can become when you tap into the power of the woman.

After God had created each section of life, He declared that what He created was good. There was never a mention of something "**NOT**" being good until He sees Adam's (man's) condition in the garden.

God created light and saw that it was good, then made the earth and the ocean; said it was good; made plants, trees, the sun, moon, and said this was good. He created the sea animals, birds, every kind of cattle, reptile, and bug and said this was good. Then he made man and said this was good. Then, for the first time in creation God decided that something was not good: And the Lord God said, "It is **NOT GOOD** that the man should be alone: I will make him an **HELP** meet for him" (Genesis 2:18 KJV).

Now I need to quiet the critics. I have heard some people say "man had the woman inside of him, so he was already complete, or the man had everything he needed and would have been alright by himself." If this were the case God would not have done anything else but leave woman inside of man; because after all, He is sovereign, and He does know what is best for our lives. This was not the case, so God displayed his love to man by bringing the woman into this realm.

*The **Lord God** caused a deep sleep to fall upon Adam, and he slept: and he took one of his ribs, and closed up the flesh thereof; And the rib, which the Lord God had taken from man, made him woman, and brought her unto the man. And Adam said, this is now **BONE** of my **BONES**, and **FLESH** of my **FLESH**; she shall be called Woman, because she was **TAKEN OUT** of man (Genesis 2:18 KJV).*

You have always been **GOOD**!

You were created to **fulfill** what was **not good** in the earth. This is your very reason for entering the earth realm. God has never had any other thought about you besides goodness. He created you to bring **goodness** back into his language. You are the last thing He created before resting and you are **good**. This is God's perspective towards you.

DECLARATION

I AM GOOD

GIFT

One definition of a gift is something given voluntarily without payment in return, as to show favor toward someone, honor an occasion, or make a gesture of assistance. The woman was given to man out of God's love for man, to show him favor, honor him, and give him assistance. The woman was created as a **perfect help** to the man, and her entire purpose was to help man. I want to reiterate that she is such a perfect **gift** that God **rested** after creating her.

Adam also shared the same sentiments in regards to the female; he is so excited about the **gift** he receives he declares that she is one with him. This is the pleasure that you brought into the earth! You should never consider yourself to be **ANYTHING** less than what God declares you to be.

GOLDEN NUGGETS

- A man who does not recognize he is in need of **help** will **miss** innumerable treasures in life.

- A man who does not recognize the woman was created to help him is in **serious** trouble.

- Only a **fool** will abuse or misuse his help.

- A woman who does not recognize she was created as a perfect help will miss her **true value**.

- Women **MUST** come back into their true identity, so they can help us (men) with our understanding, so we can come up to a better level of kingdom living (becoming a bride).

Any man, country, or institution that abuses the woman abuses himself!

DECLARATION

I AM A GIFT!

DEFINITION/POSITION

Many hours of research and debate have occurred about women who struggle in the area of staying in abusive relationships. I've had numerous conversations over the years with individuals concerning women who stay in abusive relationships. There appears to be a common thread among those women who navigate to and attract negative (poison) type personalities. Women who are struggling in this arena of life have wrong definitions of themselves. Well, most people would argue and say "Rob, that's common sense". Well if this is such common knowledge why do women continually find themselves in these situations?

The answer has been staring us right in the face all the time: A woman who does not understand her true identity will **automatically** stay with "bad" men due to the natural order of design. The female had **NO** definition until Adam woke up from his surgery.

I need you to check out how God set things up; "God took the Man and set him down in the Garden of Eden to **work the ground** and **keep it in order** (Genesis 2:15 MSG). So let's kill all of the controversy surrounding responsibility for the fall; from the beginning man was given the responsibility to keep things in order.

Next, God commanded the man, "you can eat from any tree in the garden except the Tree-of-Knowledge-of Good-and-Evil. Don't eat from it. The moment you eat from that tree, you're dead." (Genesis 2:16-17 MSG).

The commandment was given to the man **prior** to the woman entering the earth realm, so any communication concerning this command would come to the woman from man. Now, to examine the extent to which we have gone astray on this topic lets look at this detailed account of creation; after Adam receives the commandment God said; "its not good for the man to be alone I'll make him a helper, a companion (Genesis 2:18 MSG). We stop right here, so the typical thought process becomes that the woman was created right after God made that statement, but this is **NOT** how it happens.

After God had made the statement, the next thing He did was to empower man with the authority to give whatever created identity; "So God formed from the dirt of the ground all the animals of the field and all the birds of the air. He brought them to the Man to see what he would name them. Whatever the Man called each living creature, **THAT WAS ITS NAME** (Genesis 2:19)!

> **Then:** God put the man into a DEEP sleep. As he slept He removed one of his ribs and replaced it with flesh. God then used the rib He had taken from the man to make the woman and presented her to the man (Genesis 21-22 Message Bible).

The problem for us is that we have read this verse similar to the way we watch a movie; we don't take into account chronology of events or the time between deep sleep and awake. Female was on the scene for some time without definition; she knew that she existed, but did not know what she was, or why she was created until she was presented to the man.

Now I know this generation has a strong focus on individuality and the independent woman; I believe this is one of the primary reasons we try to dismiss the concept above, but identity is such a part of man that he also carries identity in him; it is the male who determines the gender (identity) of a child.

With this concept in mind, it becomes quite obvious that a woman will look to get her definition from a man. There's only one problem with this; because of the "fall" she will receive definitions that don't line up with God's definition of her.

GOLDEN NUGGETS

- Until a woman understands the natural order of design is to look for definition from man's point of view, she will continue having the "can't help its" when it comes to discovering her identity

- The only way to get a **correct** definition of yourself is through the eyes of Christ (second Adam)

BONE OF BONE

The first words ever spoken to female were; you are bone of bone. This statement was exhilarating to the woman. Bone is the substance that **FORMS** the body. It also serves as a storage area for calcium playing a large role in calcium **BALANCE**, in the blood. The 206 bones in the body serve several other purposes. They **SUPPORT** and **PROTECT** internal organs. Muscles pull against the bones, to make the body **MOVE**. Bone marrow, the soft, spongy tissue in the center of many bones, make and store blood cells.

The first Female was given a great image of herself. The first definitions ever declared over female is that she forms and brings balance to man. She would support and protect his "delicate" parts; she would move him. This definition brought such excitement to the woman that she was fully confident in her importance to the man's make up. The woman who begins to understand her true, primary, definition becomes empowered and does not settle for anyone who will describe, or treat her less than bone of bone.

(**Note**) There is spiritual relevance to the muscles attaching to the "**bones**" causing movement. It is very evident that there are a greater number of women (presently) in the body of Christ comparably to men. I am not surprise by this, and it is my sincere belief that there would be no "**movement**" in the church (and in the world) if it had not been for the women whom have labored diligently to keep us afloat.

41

Simultaneously, women have experienced persecution by the "spiritual" leaders, who exploited them under the guise that they were "second" place entities.

Out of all people whom have been treated as "slaves"; women in the world have been enslaved at an unprecedented rate. The Body of Christ is also guilty of this practice. Men "**WE MUST REPENT!**" God is not mocked, and we cannot move forward until we become a part of restoring women back to their original purpose. I call on all men exposed to this knowledge to repent; especially if you consider yourself to be an appropriate male or a believer.

GOLDEN NUGGETS

- Women **form**

- Women bring **balance**

- Women **support** and **protect**

- Women **move**

Women: you were designed to help form man, bring balance in him, and protect and support the internal parts of him.

THIS IS THE PRIMARY DEFINITION OF FEMALE!

I FORM

I BRING BALANCE

I SUPPORT AND PROTECT

I CAUSE MOVEMENT

FLESH

The second part of the definition given to the female is just as dynamic as the first; Adam declares that she is **FLESH** of his **FLESH**. The definition of "flesh" is the soft tissue of the body of a vertebrate, covering the bones and consisting mainly of skeletal muscle and fat.

Now imagine not having any flesh; anything that touches any part of your body not having skin covering is very painful. This is the tragedy for men who don't understand this concept. The woman is supposed to soften us up; especially in the area of relationships. They normally have the manual to a healthy relationship, and are in tuned to how they want to be treated.

In his God identity, Adam stated that the woman is the soft part of him and that she would cover him with softness. Is it not surprising that a woman always brings a softer touch to any event? In her initial design, part of her being a **"perfect"** help was to bring softness to man.

GOLDEN NUGGETS

- Women are the **soft** part of men

- She **covers** with softness

- She balances with softness

The Woman was created to cover man with a soft, balancing touch!

DECLARATION

I AM THE SOFT PART OF MAN

I COVER WITH SOFTNESS

I BALANCE WITH SOFTNESS

WOMAN

The last thing declared over the female was her **position**; Adam states that she shall be called woman BECUASE she is taken out of him! He recognizes her position and declares that she came from inside of him; she came from the core of who he is. God reached into man and pulled out what was perfect in man, for man.

He did not say she shall walk behind me or at my side, but he declared that they walked as one. I have to admit this was not a position I took in my prior relationships, which I now believe played a major role in the relationships not being successful.

I forgot that that the woman was my gift, and the many components of the gift often made me view my woman in a way which is not God ordained. I am so glad for God's forgiveness and grace which is teaching me these truths. One of the ways in which I plan to get even with the enemy is by helping men see the gift God has given us, and the exact way in which He expects us to view women. I also want women to understand how valuable they are to men.

DECLARATION

I AM BONE OF BONE

I AM FLESH OF FLESH

I AM WOMAN

TRICKSTER

Now that we have looked at the original purpose and design of women you are probably thinking "what happened?" The answer is there was a trickster in the garden who wanted to alter God's creation, and he studied humankind long enough to find an opening.

*Now the serpent was more subtle than any beast of the field which the Lord God had made. And he said unto the woman, Yea hath God said; ye shall not eat of every tree of the garden (**Genesis 3:1 KJV**)?*

Now, this verse of scripture has been the foundation of much controversy especially with regard to women. This passage has been used to declare women as weak, foolish, and lustful. Rarely has this verse been used to declare the woman's genuine desire.

I asked the Holy Spirit this question; why was the devil successful at appealing to the woman? Did he appeal to her Flesh? Well sin had not entered the world at that time, so I can't say she was being flesh driven with 100% confidence. Was it lust of the Eyes? We do have evidence of the fruit looking pleasant, but she had seen that fruit all the time yet never ate it before just because it looked good.

There had to be some focus on the tree, because it was known to be a tree to be avoided. Was it the Pride of Life? Well, we could argue this point; she was seeking to be something, but that is still debatable. There is only one reason that the enemy was successful at tricking the woman; he appealed to her desire to be more like God.

50

The devil said, "and ye shall be as gods." I would have to say after analyzing this passage very carefully, if the woman is "**lusting**" after anything she is "**lusting**" after God! I know that by making this statement I will face attacks by those who want to keep women in their "place". They will use some theological point to bring the focus back to some weakness in the woman, but study the scriptures yourself and then draw your own conclusions.

The devil tricked her, not because she was weak, stupid, or had some other deficiency as it has been preached in thousands of sermons: she was legitimately tricked! The devil used all of his characteristics to fool her into believing a lie. He convinced her that she would be just like God.

So then the question becomes; what would make the woman not already know she was made in the image of God? Once again the answer has been starring us directly in the face; we have just failed to use the brilliant deductive reasoning we have been blessed with, and have not seen with our spiritual eyes.

The last thing created on earth was the woman; she was not a part of naming anything, and she got her identity and position directly from the man. She received her instruction with regards to functioning from him also. God gave the man his identity, so it would be evident that the man would most likely be in tune with his likeness to God. I would have to surmise that since the woman got her identity and position from the man, she would be more in tune with her likeness to him rather than God.

This is the reason the devil came at the woman; he knew that he had an advantage with regards to her identifying more with the **man** opposed to **God**.

51

This is also the reason I believe nothing happened until Adam ate the fruit; the man was **NOT** deceived, but the woman **WAS** deceived. The enemy used his ability of "subtleness" to grasp the woman's curiosity and then got her to question her identity. The primary definition of subtle is **elusive**: it means difficult to **detect** or **grasp** by the mind or **analyze**. So, it was not a decision the devil presented to the woman, and she simply took the bait; he presented it in a way that made it difficult for her to grasp, detect, and analyze.

GOLDEN NUGGETS

- The woman in essence was trying to become **"spiritual"**

- The woman began questioning her **image** due to the **elusiveness** of the enemy

- Anytime you **listen** to the enemy you will begin to **question** your **image** (who you are)!

THE STRUGGLE

A series of events began that would put discord between the man and woman. The man in his "fallen" condition would look at his **gift** differently and begin using her as a focus of **blame** opposed to seeing her as a gift or helper. Women in many instances are still receiving blame for men's failures today.

*"And the man said, the **woman** whom thou gavest to be with me, she gave me of the tree, and I did eat" (**Genesis 3:12 KJV**).*

When God questioned Adam, he blamed his gift. Of course, the woman had some influence on him, but he was responsible for speaking to the serpent, or her, with regards to her image: why? He was the one who declared her identity to her in the first place.

This is an important insight for men who want to have rewarding relationships; it is also very important for men who have daughters. We are either giving identity or blame to the women in our lives, so make sure you are careful about your choice. If you choose correctly then blessings will pour into your life. If you make any other choice, it will result in a form of negativity which will make wish you had chosen differently.

EVE IDENTITY

The following concept is going to be very hard for many to swallow, but I hope you can grasp the revelation that is about to be exposed to you. The name EVE is a "fallen" identity. Let me take you back to a verse of scripture examined in the beginning; whatever the Man called each living creature, **THAT WAS ITS NAME** (Genesis 2:19)!

When Adam initially spoke to the woman, he spoke from a "light" perspective, so he named her something exhilarating. Her identity and functioning came from the name, and she was confident that she was someone special. But, after the fall Adam decided that he would rename the woman. Now, Adam gave her the name Eve, which means mother of life, but she was always designed to be the mother of all.

This is very evident by the fact that she was not supposed bear children in pain, but she was always destined to bear children. Adam no longer had light; thus he began to speak from a dark identity reflected by darkness "eve." The devil had succeeded in his quest to mess the man and the woman up.

If you examine the scriptures, you will find that God never called the woman by the name "Eve". Even when questioning the events of the fall, God still called her "Woman." Why is this? The woman never lost any value in God's eyesight.

TWISTED IMAGE

As a human, you either operate from kingdom principles or you are effected by "fallen" principles. There is no getting around it. Just because you may not be a believer, the principles of God do not change. God informed the woman of how the fallen condition would affect her; **SHE WAS NOT CURSED**! Go examine the scriptures for yourself; God cursed the serpent and the ground, **NOT THE WOMAN** or **MAN**!

God told the Woman *"I'll multiply you pains in childbirth; you'll give birth to your babies in pain. You'll want to please your husband but he'll lord it over you" (Genesis 3:16 KJV)*

Yes, there are clear consequences because of the woman's choice, but she was not cursed. Not only would she now get natural pain where there should not have been, but she would no longer enjoy a favorable view in the man's eyesight. "Fallen" state women (**those without Christ**) spend their time making babies (in pain) trying to "satisfy" men who are domineering (lord), and trying to understand why they are not accepted. I call this operating from **Eve Identity**!

There is also spiritual relevance to this; every dream, idea, inspiration (babies) will be unrealized and dictated by men (lord) and you will always be put in your "place"; when you function from your fallen (Eve) identity opposed to your resurrected or redeemed identity.

GOLDEN NUGGETS

- A woman **WITHOUT** Christ will spend her time operating from Eve identity; she will waste time trying to get her definition and direction from **A** man opposed to **THE MAN** (Christ)

- Women are key to what's going to happen next in the kingdom

- "Fallen" state women (**those without Christ**) will spend their time making babies, trying to satisfy men who are domineering, and trying to understand why they are not accepted.

- Every dream, idea, and inspiration will be unrealized and dictated to you by a man when you function from your fallen "Eve" identity opposed to your resurrected or redeemed identity.

- God wants to use what the devil did to try to destroy your identity to make a **TOTAL** mockery out of the devil!

FEMINIST MOVEMENT

Would you say that you were righteous if you cursed your child because she or he got fooled? I don't believe that you would take that stance, but we have operated from this perspective for so long that it has hurt women and men.

If we don't begin to change our mindset concerning this concept we will not enjoy the full benefits of the perfect help created for men, or the redemptive work Christ did for us in restoring our "perfect" help. Women, it is time for you to move beyond the fallen perception that the enemy tried to give you because **WE NEED YOUR HELP!**

Women encourage beliefs like empathy, value, agreement, acceptance of differing views, and empowerment. You must come into your "original" identity so that we can move forward together to our "dynamic" destiny.

In addition to this, somebody got it wrong when they documented that the feminist movement started in the 18th or 19th Century: The "**Women's Movement**" began in Genesis 3:15. The wonderful thing about God is He loves us so much, that He will use the exact thing the devil tried to use to destroy us and make a mockery of the devil.

God declares that He is not only going to use the Woman's seed and make a mockery of the devil; He's going to take His church and crown it with a definition that truly exemplifies a woman in her most beautiful moment. He said to the devil "**I'M GOING TO CALL HER MY BRIDE**" as an eternal reminder (devil) that I am getting even with you for tricking my perfect creation.

ENMITY

*"And the Lord God said unto the serpent, Because thou hast done this, thou art cursed above all cattle, and above every beast of the field; upon thy belly shalt thy go, and dust shalt thou eat all the days of thy life: And I will put **enmity** between thee and the woman, and between thy seed and her seed; it shall bruise thy head and thou shalt bruise his heel" (Genesis 3:14-15 KJV)*

The definition of enmity is:
- A state of **deep-seated** ill-will

- **Mutual** hatred or ill will

- The bitter **Attitude** or **Feelings** of an enemy or of mutual enemies; hostility; antagonism

- A feeling or **Condition** of hostility; hatred; ill will; animosity; antagonism

The Message Bible is clear, God says to the devil; I'm declaring **WAR** between you and Woman, between your offspring and hers. He'll (Jesus) wound your head, and you'll wound his heel.

WOMAN WARRIOR

When I'm speaking to women I often ask this question "how many of you feel as though you are in a war?" The hands go up, and the answer is the same. Then I ask "how many of you know that God put you in a war?" Most of them look at me like I have three heads and seven eyes. Then I show them: God **cursed** the **serpent** and the **ground**, but He declared war (**enmity**) between the **woman** and the **serpent**, between his offspring and her offspring. God said that the woman would be the conduit that He uses to tear the devil's entire kingdom down.

You are a woman warrior designed to win! This is God's perfect redeemed plan for you. He made this promise to you in Genesis, and I will show you how He fulfilled it in the book of John. God never meant for you to settle for a lower image of yourself; He wanted you to beat the devil in the head every chance you got.

But, there is one thing you must know:

YOU CANNOT WIN THE WAR AGAINST THE DEVIL OUTSIDE OF HAVING A RELATIONSHIP WITH CHRIST!

There are two key systems in a war; military or civilian; you are either one or the other. The major difference between the two is one system has the equipment to fight and the other does not. There is nothing more horrendous than being civilian casualties. You rarely hear about them, and they are never celebrated on the news for heroic behavior or anything else, but they still give their lives in war.

If you don't come into your identity in Christ, you have no choice but to get beat up by your enemy. Your adversary will do anything to keep you away from the knowledge of your true identity. Because you are in a war, you must gear up for the battle. There is only one way to win, and that is through your authority in Christ. A woman who understands her identity in Christ will become as powerful as a nuclear weapon to the devil's kingdom: and he is frightened to death about her coming into her true identity.

GOLDEN NUGGETS

- A Woman who comes into her image in Christ will have the ability to **crush** the devil!

- The only way to your "true" identity is through the eyes of Christ!

DECLARATION

I AM A WOMAN WARRIOR DESIGNED TO WIN!

RESTORED IDENTITY

I want to take you back to a statement I made earlier; (1) God made a **declaration** over the woman; (2) God never designed the woman to have a second place citizenship. Jesus came to fulfill the promise made in Genesis. He also made sure the woman would know that her identity had been restored, and she no longer had to live with blame or shame from what happened in the Garden of Eden.

*And when they wanted wine, the mother of Jesus saith unto him, they have no wine. Jesus saith unto her "**Woman**, what have I to do with thee? Mine hour is not yet come" (John 2:3-4 KJV).*

Sometimes the Holy Spirit will draw our attention to verses of scripture and then ask us questions. If God asks a question, He already knows the answer, so it becomes evident that He is giving you a clue into His mindset on the subject. He posed this question to me "why would Jesus speak to his mother in a manner that seemed disrespectful?"

This question spoke to me because I was raised to respect my mother, and I could imagine getting the "right" response if I call my mother "woman", no matter how old I am (if you were born before the 80's you will know "exactly" what I mean, if not, ask someone). Out of all people in the world Jesus would still be a gentleman, especially to his mother.

Some have debated that this was the manner in which men spoke to all women in those days, but the Holy Spirit showed me something different, confirmed it further on in the scriptures, and since then I have been convinced of this concept.

The Woman spoke to Jesus out of her "true" identity, and He was answering her prophetically. He was in essence saying I have not completed the process of restoring you to your "complete" identity, so why are you speaking to me in your warrior identity? I haven't finished the job!

Mary was speaking prophetically in her true image which is defined in Christ. This began the public declaration of the promise made to the woman in the Garden:

And I will put **enmity** *between thee and the woman, and between thy seed and her seed; it shall bruise thy head and thou shalt bruise his heel" (Genesis 3:14-15 KJV)*

Woman had tapped into her promise and identity, which is defined in Christ. She was being restored to the initial design and destiny that God had ordained for her from the beginning of time. She was declaring prophetically that her time had come, and I can prove it: **Jesus complied with her request!**

If, He had nothing to do with her or was being disrespectful, He would have just gone about his business. The **Woman** was standing up in her God given identity, so Jesus had to respond.

COMPLETING THE PROMISE

Jesus would complete the promise and fulfill what God declared to the **woman** in the book of beginnings. She would no longer have to feel as though she had a "second-class" citizenship. He would take the blame and shame away that had been a source of distress to her for over 2000 years.

*When Jesus therefore saw his mother, and the disciple standing by, whom he loved, he saith unto his mother, "**Woman**, behold thy son!" (John 19:26)*

Now, many people have given sermons about this scripture, but they focus on Jesus making sure He took care of His mother. I do believe this was a factor, but there was a larger revelation to the statement; it was a declaration of "full" restoration, "Woman behold thy son!" **Woman** behold your **SEED** who has crushed the devil's plan against you!

He was declaring that the promise had been completed; He was speaking prophetically to her as she had fully regained her identity. The promise had been fulfilled. She had been restored to her **ORIGINAL** state.

God has a wonderful plan and purpose for you; one that is not centered on a lower level of living, disappointment, and struggle. God's plan for your life is one that is full of peace, joy, and strength. He has visited you throughout the BIBLE and has restored your identity through Jesus Christ; now is the time for you to walk in your destiny!

GOD'S DESIGN

Whether you are a believer or not your heavenly father designed you with greatness. He saw what was needed in the earth, reached into man, and pulled you out. His plan for you is wonderful, and he allowed me to write this book just to remind you of how important you are.

Women: You are **GOOD**; you are **GIFTS**; you give **FORM**; you bring **BALANCE**; you **SUPPORT** and **PROTECT** internal parts; you cause **MOVEMENT**. You are the **SOFT** part of man. You **COVER** with **SOFTNESS**; you are **BONE** of **BONE** and **FLESH** of **FLESH**:

You are WOMEN WARRIORS DESIGNED TO WIN!

- He declared her a **WARRIOR** in Genesis 3:15
- He made her **LAUGH** at death in Gen 21:1-7
- He gave her **PRAISE** in Gen 29:35
- He stop fighting and gave her a **RULER** in Gen 30
- He gave her a **DELIVERER** in Exodus 2
- He gave her a **SOJOURNER** in Exodus 18:3, 4 (To reside temporarily, A temporary stay; a brief period of residence, cause this isn't your final destination)
- He gave her an **INHERITANCE** in Num 27
- He took her out of prostitution, and made her the salvation for her entire family in Joshua 6:22 (your **PAST** is not your **FUTURE**), Heb 11:31 (**HALL OF FAITH**) why did he not change her status; it's a statement to the world that former status does not dictate your destiny
- He made her a **LEADER** in Judges 4:4
- He gave her a **SAMSON** in Judges 13:2
- He gave her a **MILLIONAIRE** in Ruth 4:13
- He gave her a **MIGHTY PROPHET** in 1 Sam 20
- He gave her **RESTORATION** in 1 King 1:46
- He gave her **WISDOM** in 1 Kings 10:6

- He gave her **BACK** her son in 1 Kings 17:22 (PARK HERE)
- He made her a **QUEEN** in Esther 2:17
- He **DECLARES** that she is **VIRTUOUS** in Proverb 31:10
- He named her Ecclesiastes **CALLED OUT ONES**
- Then he sung her **SONGS** in song of Solomon
- In Hosea he gave her a righteous man **DESPITE** of her sin
- And took her **BACK AGAIN** when she forgot his grace in Hosea 3
- Called her **DAUGHTER OF ZION** in Zephaniah 3:14
- He **CHECKED** the men on the treatment of her in Malachi 2:14
- He declared that she was **BLESSED** and **HIGHLY FAVORED** in Matt 1:18
- He called her **DAUGHTER**, healed her of her issues, and made her **WHOLE** in Mark 5:34
- He delivered her daughter despite her not being a part of the "**CLICK**" in Mark 7:29
- He declared the widow as a more **EXTRAVAGANT** giver in Mark 12:44
- He declared that **HER STORY** would be told alongside the Gospel in Mark 14:9

- He appeared to her **FIRST** in Mark 16:9
- He gave her the **FIRST** experience of being **FILLED** with the Holy Ghost Luke 1:41
- He had **COMPASSION** on her in Luke 7:13
- He **VALIDATED** her in Luke 7:50
- He gave her **COMFORT** in Luke 8:48
- And He **WOULDN'T TAKE THE GOOD PART** from her in Luke 10:42
- He **LOOSED** her in Luke 13:12
- He **CALLED HER BACK** to her true identity in John 2:4
- He **FILLED** her thirst in John 4:29
- He her gave **CREDABILITY** in John 4:39
- He **WOULDN'T CONDEMN** her in John 8:11
- He **RAISED HER** brother from the dead in John 11:43
- He made them **LEAVE HER ALONE** in John 12:7

And in Rev 22:17 the **BRIDE** says come

YOU
ARE
WOMAN!

To purchase a copy of the book or if you are interested in a presentation contact:

Robert C Bennett
P.O 1971
Niagara Falls, NY 14302

Or

fbeenit2@comF5.com

Also contact me on facebook

Look for other books by Robert C Bennett:

Letters to the Women I Love

17975630R00044

Made in the USA
Middletown, DE
16 February 2015